IMAGES OF IRELAND

EDENDERRY

IMAGES OF IRELAND

EDENDERRY

EDENDERRY HISTORICAL SOCIETY

NONSUCH

To the people of Edenderry and in particular all those who have been associated with the Edenderry Historical Society.

First published 2009

Nonsuch Publishing
119 Lower Baggot Street
Dublin 2
Ireland
www.nonsuchireland.com

British Library Cataloguing in Publication Data.
A catalogue record for this book is available from the British Library.

ISBN 978 1 84588 957 9

Typesetting and origination by Nonsuch Publishing
Printed by Athenaeum Press

Contents

Young boys gather to watch the aftermath of the fire at O'Brien's Universal Providing Stores in August 1955.

Covered in snow and peaceful. This building was at one time a schoolhouse for the local Quaker community.

Introduction

This pictorial history of Edenderry in the twentieth century is a sample of the people, places and events of the past one hundred years. It is a treasure of memories and reminiscences for the people of the 'Brow of the Oaks'. This project is evidence of the sterling work done by the Edenderry Historical Society since its formation in 1979. In February 2008 several members voiced their enthusiasm for such a project, conscious of the precarious nature of some of the images available. They believed that now was the time for such a production lest many of the images be lost or destroyed. To all who gave freely of their time, stories and most importantly the images, a sincere debt of gratitude is offered. The contributors are as follows: Patience Pollard; Tommy Wall; Paula Lalor; Oliver Burke; Catherine Watson; Angela Tedders; Francis Rowe; Mary Fay; Nan Usher; Michael Byrne; John Kearney and the staff of the Offaly Historical and Archaeological Society Research Centre in Tullamore; Hugh O'Donaghue; Peggy Farrell; Seamus Rafferty; Bridge Greer; Fr P.J. McEvoy; Seán Farrell; Monica Nolan; Kathleen Kelly; Ciarán Reilly; Frank Caffery; Doris and Seamus O'Connor; Eileen Hickey; Therese Abbot; Mary Haughton; Margaret Smullen; Mrs McInerney; Phyllis Tyrell; Mary Fayne; Maurice O'Regan; Liam Moran; Mary O'Connor; Des Farrell; Joan Cronin; Mairead Evans; Declan O'Connor; Aine Usher, and Noel Farrelly. Each and every one of the above have made this production possible.

Catherine Watson, Mairead Evans, Therese Abbott, Eileen Hickey, and Patience Pollard, who were on hand when the material was being gathered and collated, deserve warmest thanks for their endeavours. Likewise the staff of Edenderry Library, in particular Martina Mooney and Noreen Owens for their unstinting support throughout and for allowing us the use of the premises to meet and copy photographs. A special thank you to Aisling O'Kelly, whose innovation and foresight greatly enhanced this project. Similarly to Ciara Nally for her expertise in enhancing the quality of the images when called upon. Edenderry Historical Society is thankful to Nonsuch for including this book in their *Images of Ireland* series and the assistance provided by Mr Ronan Colgan and Stephanie Boner.

The collection includes wonderful memories of the past such as Alesbury's, O'Brien's, 'The Big Freeze of '47', Cardinal Gilroy, and the old streetscape. Some important figures such as Charles Manners, a town clerk from the early part of the century, are included, but in the main this book tells the story of ordinary people of Edenderry. Like any history, it is but a sample of

McDermott's barge is stuck in ice during 'The Big Freeze of 1947', close to the Downshire Bridge.

times past. I have enjoyed copying each and every photograph, coupled with the sharing of memories from days long past, from Eileen Hickey's reminiscences of the Mass in Monasteroris in 1929 celebrating the centenary of Catholic Emancipation, and recollections of men such as Michael McInerney driving cattle through the town's main street for Francie Dunne, to Liam Moran's memories of dances and balls in the town hall in the 1950s.

This book is the product of a great deal of work from the Edenderry Historical Society. Over fifty people have been involved in producing this book. However I would like to pay particular mention to Mairead Evans whose ingenuity in the first place spurred this publication from humble beginnings. Her willingness, love of Edenderry and ever cheery spirit is an inspiration to us all. As the Edenderry Historical Society enters its thirtieth year we hope that it will be celebrated and that the endeavours of its members, including those no longer with us, will be remembered by all.

Ciarán Reilly, Chairperson Edenderry Historical Society 2008
and Cherry Carter, Chairperson Edenderry Historical Society 2009.

Edenderry Historical Society 1979-2009

On the 23 January 1979 at a meeting in St Joseph's Hall (Old Boys' School), Edenderry Historical Society was formed. Elected as officers on this occasion were Tom Ryan as Chairperson (currently Treasurer), May Patterson as Vice-Chairperson, Michael Moore as Secretary, Hubert Merrick as Treasurer and Michael Collins as P.R.O., while Archdeacon Finney acted as the

Patron of the Society. The meeting resolved that where and when possible, research would be carried out by its members into the various aspects of Edenderry's past, which included the workhouse, the Quakers, the Grand Canal, Monasteroris Friary and the Downshire connection. Thirty years later, all of those aims and more have been successfully completed by the society.

Over the years the society has been very active and between 1983 and 1986 it was involved in reading the headstones in the graveyards at Drumcooley, Ballinakill, Ballymacwilliam, Castro Petre, the Society of Friends and Shean. In 1991 a publication called *Edenderry Then and Now* listed all the graves that the society had recorded, a valuable source for genealogy and those looking to trace information about their ancestors. The society has always received requests for information from people with Edenderry connections, indeed even in the past twelve months requests have come from Canada, the United States, England, Scotland, Australia and New Zealand. In 1989 Seán McBride, winner of the Noble Peace Prize unveiled a monument to the Wexford rebels, Revd Mogue Kearns and Col. Anthony Perry at the site of the execution in Blundell Wood in 1798. The highlight for the members of the historical society during the past thirty years came in 1998 when the bicentenary of the 1798 Rebellion was celebrated with a weekend of activity in July of that year, including a commemorative pageant and a parade to Monasteroris graveyard.

Numerous publications since have filled in the blanks and the history of Edenderry is well documented by members of the society. Mairead Evans, a former school teacher, has traced the history of the Grand Canal in her book *Safe Harbour*, while Mairead with the late Noel Whelan, Librarian, wrote the pamphlet *History of Edenderry* in 2000, which outlines some of the major events at Edenderry and which proved to be a useful starting point for other research. The contribution of the late Noel Whelan is one which the members of the society are acutely aware of. He did sterling work in the short years that we were all blessed to have shared with him. Society member Therese Abbott has carefully carried out research on the Quakers of Edenderry who were so prominent in the town for almost 200 years. Recently Ciarán Reilly, has written two books, *Edenderry County Offaly and the Downshire estate 1790-1800* and *Edenderry 1820-1920: popular politics and Downshire rule*, which look at the involvement of the Downshire family, owners of Edenderry from 1786 to 1922.

Current projects include further recording of the graveyards, into those not featured in the 1991 edition, which is being carried out by Therese Abbott and Mary Fay. It his hoped that their publication *Carved in Stone* will be available in the near future. For many, an annual highlight has been the trip which takes place on the May Bank Holiday weekend. Places visited so far and under the brilliant guide of Hugh Smyth include Cork, Mayo, Derry, and Donegal. Lectures are delivered to the society by historians from all across the country monthly from September to April. The society welcomes speakers and those willing to give a lecture, or indeed any correspondence. Contact can be made at edenderryhistory@gmail.com.

Members of Edenderry pipe band pass along JKL Street during an Easter commemoration.

'The Lodge' located on the Carrick Road was demolished in 1994. It is thought locally to have been used by either the local Orange Lodge or the Masonic Order.

Newspaper Articles

Irish Independent, 18 June 1935

Edenderry Shoe Factory – Big Premises Opened

The Edenderry Shoe Company (Messrs Wachman and Co.) was informally opened today when twenty young natives of the district were taken on for training. Before the end of the week 100 youths, boys and girls will be engaged. Twenty-five expert operatives from Leicester have been sent there to instruct the employees how to use the machinery which is capable of turning out 10,000 pairs of shoes per week. It is expected that 3,000 pairs will be manufactured next week. The factory is devoted to the manufacture of ladies' shoes.

The new factory is situated in the premises formerly occupied by Messrs Alesbury Brothers Ltd which was closed about four years ago. The building which was described at the time by Senator Connolly as 'a conglomeration of afterthoughts' has been remodelled and converted into premises stated to be the best of their class in the country. The main building has a floor space of 20,000 square feet and is for the purpose of transport ideally situated beside the Grand Canal.

The latest machinery has been installed and the work of preparation which involved a huge amount of deconstruction and the installation of electric power and machinery was done in very short time. The expert operatives work will cease as the newly engaged staff acquire a knowledge of the work.

When the factory is working at full capacity employment will be given to 400 to 500 hands. Deep interest was taken in the opening of the factory today.

The Irish Times, 5 June 1941

Sad Scenes at Funerals

Business was suspended in Edenderry during the funeral of the seven members of the Browne family. People were present from all parts of the country. After requiem mass which was celebrated by Very Revd Dr Tierney PP the funeral took place in Drumcooley. Members of the LDF formed a guard of honour and fired over the grave instructed by Assistant group leader J. O'Connell. The attendance included Lieutenant C. A. Clarke, Curragh representing the

A new year is underway at St Mary's Girls' National School: Sisters Pauline, Ultan, Colmcille, Teresa Joseph, Euphrasia, Senan, Cuthbert, Claver, Marie Goretti and Oliver are pictured with Monica Foran.

Defence Forces, district leader P. Egan (North Offaly command staff of LDF), Dr McCarthy, Dr J. Farrelly, Mr G. O'Connell (Offaly county Council) and Mr J.F. Gill (ITGWU).

Tragic scenes were witnessed when the bodies of many of the bomb victims were removed from the morgue and the city hospitals. A lorry with seven coffins brought the remains of the Browne family from Dublin to Edenderry where internment later took place at Drumcooley cemetery.

The coffin of Henry (Harry) Browne who had been a member of the LDF was covered by the Tri Colour and as the lorry left the morgue a party of LDF formed under Capt W. Hamilton. Thousands of people watched the small funeral procession as it passed through the streets of the city. The chief mourners were John Corrigan, father of Mrs Browne, Daniel, Bernard and Robert Corrigan, Edward and J. Dunne (uncles), John McGlinchy brother-in-law, Seamus Kennedy (cousin), Misses Anne, Carmel and Margaret Corrigan (sisters) and Mr George O'Connell. Edenderry TC was also present.

John McGlinchy of the Crescent, Clontarf had the job of identifying the remains of the Browne family.

The Irish Times, 23 January 1945

Town Hall Gutted

Edenderry Town Hall, a massive Georgian structure was destroyed by fire early yesterday morning. Also consumed by the flames were irreplaceable cinema equipment; the complete

Looking towards the square in the 1950s.

records of Edenderry Town Commissioners; 2,000 books valued at £500 belonging to the new library located in the Town Hall; LDF records and hundreds of chairs belonging to the cinema. A courthouse equipped by the Offaly County Council was also gutted but the court records were saved. No lives were lost. Mrs O'Connell (widow) the caretaker and her seven children were sleeping on the premises and owe their lives to their little dog who roused them by barking at Mrs O'Connell's bedroom door at 6.30a.m. Finding the place full of smoke Mrs O'Connell called for help and brought the children to safety. The dog had escaped from the Civic Guard Barrack where he had been kept for some days as he was regarded dangerous to children. The huge metal dome above the roof of the hall caved in about 7.30 and the roof collapsed sending a sheet of flame and sparks into the air.

The Irish Times, 10 February 1945

Doomed Dog Saves a Family – Must 'Smokey' be Destroyed?

Just a mongrel, that's Smokey – a mongrel that chased children, cyclists and motorcars, but the pet of the O'Connell children who live with their widowed mother in Edenderry Town Hall. He got a reputation of being dangerous to children. There was no second chance; he was taken away to the local Civic Guard Barracks to be shot. Locked up in an outhouse he used all his mongrel cunning and somehow broke out and ran through the dark streets of the town to his one-time home.

But his home was in flames and he knew the children who loved him were inside. This was enough for Smokey. His barking roused Mrs O'Connell and the children – and other townsfolk, and the family got out of the building safely.

But what of the condemned dog? From a position closely resembling that of Edenderry's Public Enemy number one, he has now become the town's hero. Now they are wondering can they save him.

The Irish Times, 8 August 1955

Seven Brigades Fight Fire for Four Hours

The premises of M.P. O' Brien one of the largest general merchants on the midlands was badly damaged by fire on Saturday. Fire brigade units from Edenderry, Dublin, Navan, Maryborough, Tullamore, Kildare and the Curragh fought the flames for over four hours before bringing it under control.

Only the greatest precautions prevented the fire from spreading to nearby premises and fortunately the firemen were able to stop the flames reaching a petrol tank containing about 1,000 gallons. The central building of the large block, also a wine and spirit store, at the rear of the building was destroyed and a storage and drying plant was damaged.

The town's water supply was not sufficient to meet the demand and was augmented by running a line of hoses to the Grand Canal a quarter of a mile away.

Mr E. O'Brien, one of the directors of the company was holidaying in Glenarriff, County Antrim at the time and has returned to Edenderry to survey the damage.

Messrs M.P. O'Brien regret that owing to the fire at their main premises Edenderry there may be some slight disorganisation for a few days. Meantime grocery, hardware and the bar department will be at their adjoining premises and the general drapery departments will be opened immediately at their Arthur Williams branch, Edenderry. Van deliveries will be as usual.

Brenny Hughes delivers post to young Lynsey Alesbury, his daily routine for many years.

The Irish Times, 17 January 1989

Canal Breach Threatens Fish Life

The OPW has estimated that the breach of the Grand Canal at Edenderry, County Offaly on Sunday last has caused over £1 million worth of damage and there were growing fears last night of major pollution in the River Boyne as a result of the breach. Three square miles of farmland were still under water early yesterday morning although much of the water absorbed overnight in the Boyne which is at an abnormally low level for this time of the year. However there were fears of a fish kill in the river yesterday because of the canal water which has been treated with a weed killer Caserone G which can be lethal for fish life. It is believed that the high wind as well as an unusually high quantity of water in the stretch of the canal near Edenderry contributed to the breach in the bank. A weakness in the bed of the canal may also have been a factor. However local farmers claimed yesterday that the breach was as a result of neglect by the former owners of the canal, CIE and the OPW. One local man, Mr Patrick Moore who saved many livestock from drowning when the breach occurred said yesterday that he had been reporting the decaying state of the canal bank to both CIE and the OPW for over three years. OPW spokesperson Mr Chris Flynn has denied Mr Moore's allegations and says the bank was checked no later than last week and everything was in order. Council officials say that were it not for two culverts on the Edenderry–Rathangan road which allowed the water to flow into adjoining drains and eventually to the Boyne, the situation would have been a catastrophe. Lands belonging to the international singer Josef Locke were flooded in the breach but luckily Mr Locke had sold his livestock four days earlier. A spokesman for the OPW which is responsible for the maintenance of the canal said yesterday that the breach would take a considerable length of time to repair. OPW engineers are still surveying the damage.

Yvonne Usher's hair-dressing salon and Christy Judge's butchers.

Aerial view of O'Connell Square and the Town Hall.

Left: The Celtic Tiger has arrived in Edenderry as Nolan's Hall is pulled down to make way for new town houses.

Right: Michael Collins invokes the spirit of 1916 during the Easter commemorations.

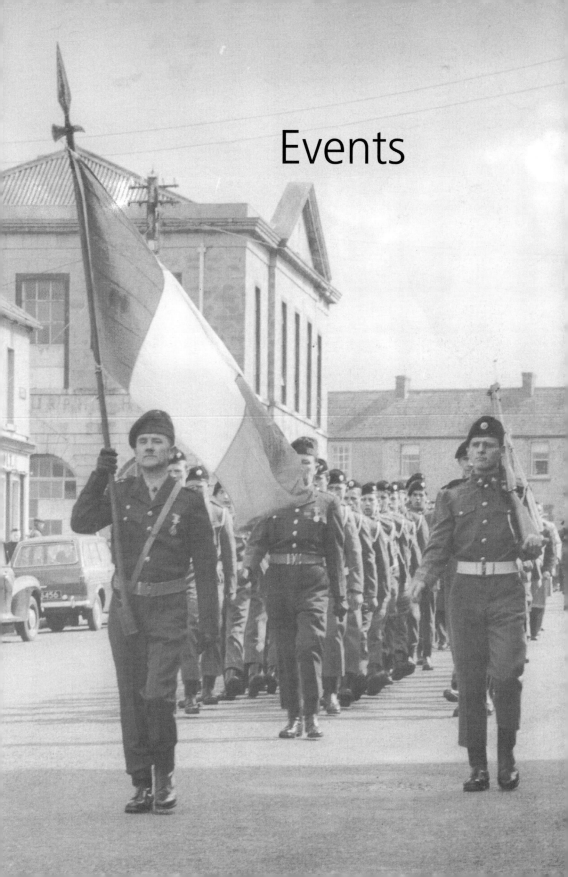

Events

Another barge is stuck at Edenderry, February 1947.

A procession moves from the Boyne Bridge and greets the arrival of President Seán T. O'Kelly in 1950.

The last barge leaves Edenderry in 1961. On board are John Mallen, James Corrigan, Kevin O'Kennedy, Desmond O'Kennedy, Joseph Gowran, George O'Connell, Philip O'Kennedy, Jack Campbell, Michael Brady Sen, Seán O'Ceallaigh, Patsy Collins and J. McDermott.

The ice begins to melt, making it possible to navigate out of Edenderry in February 1947.

Work is carried out in February 1916 to repair the breach of the Grand Canal at Edenderry.

The cut of the Grand Canal which flows into the Harbour at Edenderry, pictured here after repair work following the January 1989 breach.

A historic day. The Fay family return to Blundell House following the departure of the Black and Tans in 1921.

Denis Fay shows his wares at a market in the GAA field, early 1950s.

A scene from a festival of the 1980s along JKL Street outside the Eden Inn restaurant.

A rare image: Fr Paul Murphy at a fundraiser in 1912 for the building of St Mary's church, which he succeeded in building and having paid for before his death in 1933.

Children play at the frozen Canal harbour during the winter of 1981.

The 1962 Leinster Fleadh Ceoil was held in Edenderry. Here musicians are pictured playing at the old Methodist church or 'The Mount'.

Gerry Farrell cycling past the Town Hall after it was burned in January 1945. The dog, Smokey, was responsible for raising the alarm which saved the occupants, the O'Connell family.

Cardinal Gilroy, Bishop of Adelaide who visited Edenderry on two occasions in the 1940s and '50s. Gilroy Avenue is named in his honour.

Greg Connor surveys the breach of the canal in January 1989.

Hubert Merrick and Raymond Tedders at a market in the GAA grounds in the 1950s.

The funeral of Hugh O'Donaghue makes it way down St Mary's Road to Ballymacwilliam Cemetery in 1952. O'Donaghue had been one of the founding members of the GAA club in Edenderry in 1891.

Members of the Old IRA march to Monasteroris, 1946. Includes Tommy Cullen and James Farrelly.

James 'Ginger' Moran places a wreath on the grave of Vol. Thomas O'Connell's grave in 1946.

Included at the Old IRA commemoration in 1946 at Monasteroris are Paddy Fitzgerald, Hugh Doyle, Jimmy Mullen, James Moran, Paddy Murphy, Francie Watson, Jack Behan, Jim Farrelly, and Tommy Grehan.

Larry Frewer, Fr P.J. McEvoy and James Bennett sign the contracts for the building of St Mary's Secondary School in 1979.

Young supporters gather at Edenderry train station before a trip to Croke Park in 1962. A one-off train ran specially for the big matches at 'Croker'.

Laying of a stone at St Mary's church which was blessed by Pope John Paul when he visited Galway in September 1979. Included are Fr P.J. McEvoy, Sam Williams, Michael and Tony Hurley and the altar servers.

View along the railway track at Edenderry from the station house.

The 9th Marquis of Downshire visits Edenderry in May 2000. He is pictured here with Mairead Evans, Patience Pollard, Mary Fay, Grattan de Courcey Wheeler and Alex Dundas.

The 9th Marquis of Downshire signs the visitor book at Edenderry Library, May 2000.

Seán Norman fixes the microphone for President Mary Robinson on her visit to Edenderry, 15 June 1994.

Fianna Fáil TD for Westmeath Mary O'Rourke (then Minister for Labour) visits Edenderry Library in May 1993. She is pictured here receiving a copy of the Edenderry Historical Society's book *Edenderry Then and Now* from Patience Pollard.

Unveiling of the IRA memorial at St Mary's Cemetery at Easter 1960. Included are Des Farrell, Sonny Collins, Eddie Moran, Fr Cullen, John Kelly, Jim Farrelly, and James Morand.

Old IRA commemoration passes along JKL Street, 1960.

Firemen are busy quenching the flames of O'Brien's fire in August 1955.

Funeral of a member of the Old IRA arrives at St Mary's church in 1946.

Members of the Edenderry battalion of the Old IRA gather at the grave of Volunteer Thomas O'Connell in 1926 at Monasteroris. O'Connell was killed in a car crash in Co. Laois in 1924. He had been a commander in the Carlow Brigade of the IRA.

The 'Volley party' at Old IRA funeral in 1946 fire the salute to a former comrade.

Tommy Grehan is presented with a medal by James 'Ginger' Moran. Grehan was active in the War of Independence. He died in 1985 in the USA. Also in the photograph are J. Farrelly, P. Fitzgerald, W. Brereton, P. Cullen, T. Grehan, T. O'Shaughnessy, and H. Butler.

Group of Old IRA men at Tommy Grehan presentation. Back row: Jim Farrelly, P. Fitzgerald, W. Brereton, P. Cullen, H. Butler. Front row: J. Moran, T. Grehan, T. O'Shaughnessy.

Patience Pollard and Lord Downshire are pictured at the Church Walk in May 2000 beside the statue of the 3rd Marquis of Downshire, who died in 1845.

The arrival of the President of Ireland, Seán T. O'Kelly at St Mary's church in 1950.

Church procession of 1952 which includes the Farrelly, Moran, O'Brien and McNally families representing O'Connell Square, Perry Street, Kearns Street and Clonmullen.

Noble Peace Prize Winner Seán McBride visits Edenderry in 1989 to unveil a monument to Kearns and Perry in Blundell Wood. Pictured here at St Mary's church are Ger Connolly, Eileen O'Connor, Johnny Kane, Seán McBride, Liam Moran, Jim Flanagan, S. McBride's friend, and Damien Donaghue.

Crowds gather in disbelief as O'Brien's smoulders in August 1955.

Cattle are driven past the Town Hall, which is in ruins. It was burned in January 1945 and remained closed until 1955.

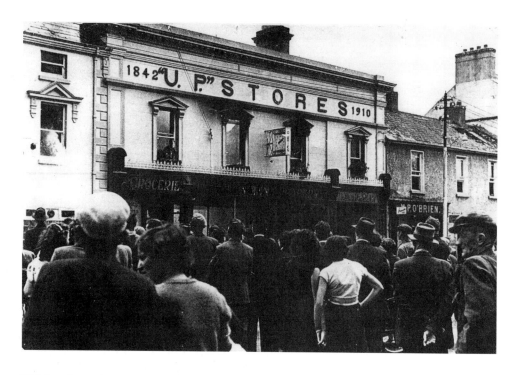

Will there be work tomorrow? Another take on the August 1955 fire at the Universal Providing Stores.

Review stand in 1950 on the occasion of President Seán T. O'Kelly's visit.

Christopher Kane is pictured in British
Army uniform during the First World
War. He survived the war and was arrested
during the War of Independence when he
was part of the local IRA battalion.

Edenderry Historical Society bicentenary commemorations of the 1798 Rebellion included a re-
enactment of the hanging in Fr Kearns and Col. Perry.

Peter Forde leads members of the Edenderry O.N.E. who took part in the bicentenary celebrations in July 1998.

Noel Whelan and Oliver Kearney play the parts of Colonel Perry and Fr Kearns during the historical society's re-enactment of the hanging of Kearns and Perry.

Joe Wyer lays a wreath in July 1998 at the grave of Fr Kearns and Col. Perry, the Wexford rebels hung and interred in Edenderry in July 1798.

Mary Robinson unveils a plaque at the Town Hall in June 1994 during her visit to Edenderry. She is pictured with historical society members Patience Pollard and Michael Collins.

'Local hero welcomed.' Seán Evans receives a hero's welcome in 1971 as he brings the Sam Maguire cup to Edenderry for the very first time. Seán is pictured here in the Harbour House with Jimmy O'Connor and supporters. For decades now the Evan's family have epitomised the spirit of the GAA.

Seán T. O'Kelly addresses the people of Edenderry during his visit of 1950. Fr Killian and Cardinal Gilroy listen on.

A float (passing the U.P.S.) and a group of young musicians from St Mary's G.N.S. make their way towards the Town Hall.

A crowd gathers outside the Town Hall for an event in the early 1950s.

Mass is celebrated at the ruins of the Franciscan Abbey at Monasteroris in 1929 to commemorate the centenary of Catholic Emancipation. Historical Society member Eileen Hickey recalls being present on this occasion.

A group of workers pause for this photograph during repairs on the breach of the Grand Canal in 1916.

Members of the Local Defence Force (LDF) from Edenderry and the surrounding area gather for review, 1941. The LDF were a volunteer group formed to protect the country during Ireland's neutrality in the Second World War.

The coffin of an LDF member is brought into Monasteroris graveyard.

A review of the LDF and the Ladies' Red Cross outside M.J. Tuohy's (now Lawless's Hardware store).

Another glance at the LDF review outside the Central Bar during the Second World War.

Peter Ford passes along the LDF review in Edenderry in the early 1940s.

Members of the Ladies' Red Cross pass along JKL Street in 1941.

The review stand of the LDF parade outside the Town Hall.

LDF parade passes along JKL Street at the Canal harbour.

The switching on of rural electrification for the townlands of Ballinakill and Ballyfore. Back Row: Garry Fitzgerald, Seán Evans, Con Forde, ESB employee, ESB employee, Ted Evans, John Crosby. Third Row: George Keane, ESB employee, Fr McWey, Fr McDonnell, Leo Poole, Oliver J. Flanagan, Fr Henry Byrne, ESB employee, Fr Tuohy, Philip Kennedy, Andy [?], Jimmy Manly, Paddy O'Connor. Second Row: Tom Evans, ESB employee, Monsignor Brenan, Jim Fay, ESB employee, Canon Maye. Front Row: Joan Cronin, Ciss Evans and Molly Evans.

A presentation on behalf of the people of the parish (Bob Evans pictured making the presentation) to Monsignor Martin Brenan to mark his Golden Jubilee as a priest. Amongst those included are: Ann Hanley, John Delamere, Martin Kearney, Finian O'Neill, Carmel Burke, Rose Corcoran, Mr Corbett, Liam Murrin, Pauric Jones, John Jones, Josephine Fanning, George Guing, Joe Tyrell, Irene Bergin, Ann Sullivan, Bernie Cummins, Marie Cummins, Mick Hurley, John Delaney, Celine McBride, Gerry Lee, Mag Denihan, Dicky Byrne, Mrs Guing, Tommy Lawton, Larry Cribbin, John Reilly, P.J. O'Sullivan, Imelda O'Meara, Joe Daly, Terry O'Mara, Kit O'Mara, Deirdre O'Mara, Ollie Loughlin, Alma Brennan, Eddie Brennan, Vera Brennan, Fr John McWey, Barbara Butler, Tom McGrath, Fr P.J. McEvoy, Gemma Denihan, Teresa Denihan, Pauric Wall, Martina Brennan, Kathleen Kane, Molly Davey, Willie Brereton, Monica Carty, Helen Young, Maura O'Callaghan, Muriel O'Callaghan, Alan Holohan, Nigel Cleary, David Denihan, Fionnula O'Callaghan, Ann Foran, Melanie Guing, Kevin Guing, Stephanie Guing, Josephine Foran, Margaret Houlihan and Martina McBride.

The funeral of the Browne family arrives in Edenderry 4 June 1941. A massive 500lb German bomb which was dropped on the North Strand, Dublin on 31 May 1941 had claimed the lives of seven members of the Browne family; Harry, his wife Molly, their four children Maureen, Ann, Edward and Angela, and Harry's mother Mary.

Harry and Molly Browne with children Ann and Maureen in happier days.

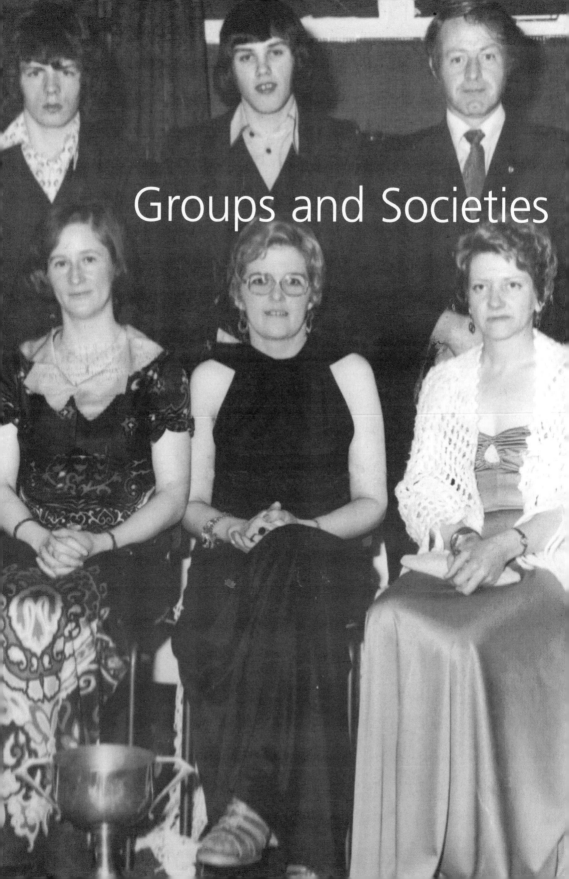

Groups and Societies

The Boyne Players were hugely popular and staged some wonderful productions over the years.

Above: A group of badminton players pictured in Nolan's Hall. Left to right: Frank Burke, Phil Hayes, Monica Nolan, Liz Farrell, Cis Maher, Mario Kelly, Seán Foran, Fr Kevin O'Neill, Michael Stynes and Liam Corcoran.

Previous page: Celebrating a victory on the badminton court are Noel Cribben, Brian Fanning, Barney McNeilis. Front row: Maureen Hickey, Cis Maher, Phil Kelly.

Bringing home the silverware to Edenderry are Badminton players who include Nancy Devine, Helen McGovern, Eddie Moran, Henry Hill and Freddie Williams.

Edenderry GAA and Golf Club Carnival, 1947. This float named 'Tourists' passes along JKL Street.

Edenderry Church Choir pictured here in the 1970s. Back row: Con Glynn, Seán Gowran, Gerry Lee, Tom O'Neill, Fr Aughney, Michael Brady, Frank Carlin, Brennie Hughes. Third row: Mary Fanning, Phil Kelly, Patsy Mangan, Jackie Kelly, Larry McDonald, Michael Collins, Seamus Butler, Henry Butler, Michael Nolan, Kathleen Fahy, Ann Marie McDermott. Second row: John Kelly, Maura Tyrell, Kathleen Callaghan, Margaret Farrell, Bernie Brady, Mary Dillon, Liz Farrell, Sheila Collins, Alice Byrne, Francis Mangan, Ita Butler. Front row: Marie Nolan, Josephine McDonnell, Mary Conlon, Sr Joan Walker, Sr Mary Curran, Evelyn McNeilis, Aileen Fitzpatrick, Carmel Farrell and Helen Comerford.

Members of the Edenderry Choir at their annual dinner in Nolan's Hall, 1956.

Cloncannon Cricket Team of the 1930s, which included Ned Shaugnessy, Tommy Hurst, Jack Homan, Barney Carroll, Richard Homan, Jimmy Usher. Front row: Paddy, Tommy, and Peter Usher; Bob Homan and Jack Holt.

Cloncannon Cricket Team. Back row: Barney Carroll, Tommy Hurst, Ned Shaugnessy, Jack Holt, T. Jenkins, Dick Homan. Front row: Peter, Tommy and Paddy Usher, Johnny Rowe and Johnny Byrne.

Left: Medal won by James Pollard, a member of the Cloncannon Cricket Team.

Right: Medal awarded to Michael Brady's mother for her service with Cumann na mBan during the War of Independence, 1919-21.

Organisers of the Edenderry Youth Club Concern Christmas Fast, 1984: Eddie Lynch, Eugene O'Brien, Fr P.J. McEvoy, Maeve O'Driscoll, Revd Canon Finney, Willie Brereton and Todd Morrissey (and Liz Brady partially hidden).

Among those present at this baby show in the Town Hall in the 1950s were Marie Mangan, John Mangan, Mrs Slattery with child, Lilly Dempsey, Gay Dempsey, Margaret O'Neill, Ger O'Neill and Ursula Dunne.

The Derries Cricket Team. Back row: Peter Farrell, John Joe Farrell, Ned Shaugnessy, Jimmy Flynn, Joe Guing and Dick Homan. Front row: Jimmy Usher, Jack Holt, Peter Rowe, Kevin O'Neill and Tom Rowe.

A wheelbarrow race through JKL Street during a carnival of the 1950s.

Edenderry Historical Society Committee for organising the visit of President Mary Robinson in June 1994. Back row: Therese Abbott, Mary Hughes, Mairead Evans and Oliver Burke. Front row: Patience Pollard, Seán O'Ceallaigh and Michael Collins.

Edenderry Lourdes Pilgrimage in 1997, the twenty-fifth anniversary of the group's first trip to Lourdes.

Members of the Edenderry Tennis Club pictured in Edgill's in the 1950s.

Members of the Edenderry District Band pictured here in the late 1930s.

Captain's Day at Edenderry Golf Club is celebrated in 1962.

The GAA and Golf Club carnival of 1947.

The cast of *Grand Old Days*, which was staged by the Edenderry drama group in 1975.

The Edenderry Hockey Club in 1925, after winning the Midland's league. Included are Charles Manners (second from the left in the back row) and Denis Fay (with trophy in the centre).

At the annual I.C.A. Dinner Dance in 1959 were Eileen O'Connor, Helen McGovern, Kathleen Kelly, and Tess O'Kennedy.

A large attendance at the annual I.C.A. Dinner Dance of 1957.

Group from Edenderry in Killarney National Park, 1957: Mrs Mangan, Jarvie (standing), Desmond Patterson, Frank Byrne, Cora O'Regan (Mangan), Mickey O'Regan.

Ladies Captain's Day at Edenderry Golf Club is celebrated in 1962.

Members of the Edenderry Local Defence Force (LDF) on parade during the Second World War in 1942. Left to right: Jack Brennan, Desmond Patterson, Tommy Judge, Thomas Cummins, Kit Williams, Kevin Nolan, Jack Kelly, Johnny Bergin and Kit Ryan.

New Year's Eve Dance in 1954 at the Church Walk. Pictured are Denise Burgess, Freddie Williams, Charlie Pollard, Olga Kelly, Harry Byrne, Nancy Lee, Carrie Owens, Mick Kelly, Annie Kelly, Barbara Owen, Mrs Gill, Audrey Madder, Betty Smith, Paul Gill, Ivan Kelly, Sylvia Green, Roy Kelly, Frank Tyrrell, Emie Kelly, [?] Foster, Billy Gill, Margaret Lewis, Phyllis Harris, Doreen Barnett, Mrs Barnett, Alice Douglas, Doris Gill, Phyllis Gill, Derek Colton.

A group from Macra na Feirme prepare to stage a play. Back row includes: Seán Coyne, Dennis Duggan, Billy Hickey. Fourth row: Brenny Foran, P.J. Hynes, Jimmy McMahon, Paddy Manley. Third row: Ger Moore, Henry Hill, Owen Wynne, Tony Furey, Jimmy Manley, Johnny King. Second row: Paudge McCluskey, Mick Byrne, Bob Evans, Jimmy Pollard, Peter Stones, Noel Hume, John Manley. Front row: Watt Nolan, Ted Evans, Liam Stones, Willie Bulfin, Joe O'Toole, Charlie Pollard.

Pictured here during the Old Age Pensioners' Christmas party in 1961 are Fr O'Sullivan, Fr J. McWey, Bishop Henry Byrne, and Monsignor Martin Brenan. Others in the background include Tommy Wall, Michael Mullins and Mick Byrne.

Tommy Wall prepares to entertain the crowd at the Old Age Pensioners' Christmas party, 1961.

Tommy Wall and Michael Mullin take a break from entertaining the guests.

The Edenderry Pioneer Group on a visit to Drogheda in the 1950s, including Bill Smyth, Mick Byrne, Willie Coyne, Terry Crampton, John Burke, Paddy Farrell, Seán Farrell, Pat Connor, Willie Carter, Bill Byrne, Tommy Shanley, Pat McDonnell, Frank Burke, Gerry Gorman and Johnny Reilly.

An Edenderry Pioneer Group visit to Dublin Airport in the 1950s. Back row: Barney Carroll, Mick Byrne, Tommy Nolan, Tommy Lawton, Tommy Shanley, Joe Gowran, Paddy Farrell, Johnny Byrne, Nancy O'Brien, [?] Walsh, Gerry Coyne, and Rosie O'Neill. Front row: Tommy Nolan, Leslie Nolan, Julia Nolan, Phyllis Nolan, Nuala Groome, Marie Ryall, Barbara Corrigan, Eda Hamilton, Mrs Gill, Mrs Burke, Ned Judge, Maura Brennan, Mary Moore.

Edenderry Historical Society group, early 1980s. Back row: Ger O'Brien, Tom Ryan, Revd Finney, Bridget Mangan, Francis Larkin, Pat Fay. Front row: Patience Pollard, May Donaghue, Mary Fay, Michael Collins, Brendan O'Callaghan. Sitting: May Patterson, Eimear O'Kennedy, Gene Pollard.

Cathal Reilly plants a tree along the Grand Canal in 1983 as part of the Edenderry Cubs. Garry Glennon holds the tree in place.

President of Ireland, Paddy Hillery meets some of the Edenderry Cubs along with Mrs Tyrell.

A group of Edenderry Cubs pictured here in the mid-1980s.

The staff at Aylesbury's Mills pictured here in 1929. Two years later the closure of the factory created considerable controversy in the area.

Edenderry Cubs in the 1980s. Adults: Jennifer Tyrrell, Monica Hurst, Geraldine McNamee, Therese Abbott, Madge Hurst. Scouts back row: Owen Emerson, Laurence McCarthy, John Kenny, Derek Pollard, Declan Ennis, Raymond Bell, David Tyrrell, Keith Bewley, Derek Carter, Mark Evans, Ross Evans, Damien Ennis. Front row: Stuart O'Regan, Brendan Hurst, David Cullen, Isaac Moriarty, Robert Snitigar, Marcus Clancy, Brian Dunne.

A group of children cheering on Edenderry Cricket Club in the 1950s.

Presentation of a cheque to Mrs Wynne, the winner of the St Mary's Secondary School draw, April 1984. Also included are K. O'Driscoll, Fr D. McDermott, P. Byrne, J. Mangan and Fr P.J. McEvoy.

Members of the Edenderry Canoe Club in the early 1980s. Left to right: Brian Carroll, Mark Staunton, Joseph Enright, Frankie Carroll, Martin O'Connor, Garrett Reilly, Mark Grennan and Ross Emerson.

Enjoying the Senior Citizens' Christmas party in the GAA Pavilion in the mid-1980s are Jim White, Marie McDonald, Mrs MacDonagh, Mary Farrell, Mrs Moore, Molly O'Donaghue, Patsy Kelly, Con Ford, Katie Shaugnessy, Bridie Kelly and Jenny Burke.

Out in style at the Edenderry Shoe Factory Annual Dance, 1962.

The members of the Edenderry St Vincent de Paul Society pictured here in the early 1980s, prior to a meeting.

The official opening of an extension to the Vocational School in 1954.

The Edenderry Historical Society visit Williamstown House, Carbury, Co. Kildare, in the early 1990s. Pictured are members Cherry Carter, Eimear O'Kennedy, Maura Kelly, Phil Davy, Peg Ryan, Bridget Kavanagh, May Conlon, Monica Foran, Ann Grattan, Reideen Dunne, Margaret Dunne, Patience Pollard, Ann Duffy, Mairead Evans, Tommy Wall, Eileen Hickey, Breda Caffery, Mary Fay, Therese Abbot, Frank Tyrell and Cis Murtagh.

Happy to pose for a photograph in the mid-1950s. Includes John Coughlan, Willie Bulfin, Frank Byrne, Michael Byrne, Enda Doyle, and Curry Holt.

A group of the Young Farmers' Club at Dublin Airport in 1950. Front row, left to right: Freddie Dunne, Kenneth Crowe, P. McCluskey, Bob Evans, Willie Bulfin, J. Pollard, Joan O'Sullivan, Annette Ennis, Aileen Hickey, Sonia Edgill, Seán Coyne, John Manley. Second row: John King, John Evans, Joe Mulligan, Michael Byrne, Christy O'Donaghue, John Coady, Peter Stones, Jimmy McMahon, Larry Hume, Victor Edgill, James Bergin, Michael Hume. Back row: B. Foran and John Mahon.

The Macra na Feirme float 'Strike on Here' passes along JKL Street during a parish festival.

Opposite: Paddy Maloney, founder of Edenderry Soccer Club in 1926, which included many of the workers of Alesbury's timber factory.

People of Edenderry

Christopher 'Kit' Kane, pictured here in the uniform of the Irish Army in the early years of the Irish Free State. Kit, like many of his generation, fought in the 'Great War' in the British Army.

For many years Francis Watson was a familiar figure to the people of Edenderry. He is pictured here outside the Medical Hall, happy with his work!

Sr Lorenzo, Fr McWey, Fr Sinnot, Fr Killian, and Mother de Chantal, pictured in the convent in 1954.

Charles Manners, town clerk of the Edenderry Town Commissioners in the early years of the twentieth century. He is pictured here on horseback c.1920.

Charles Manners resigned from the position of town clerk when the commissioners became overtly aligned with the IRA during the War of Independence. He is pictured here out hunting in Clonmullen.

Irish cyclist Alo Donegan visits Edenderry in the 1940s with an unusual bicycle. Note Moran's shop and Methodist church in the background.

The Alesbury family came from Bristol in the late 1860s and they established a successful timber factory in Edenderry. Daniel Alesbury and his family are pictured here in the 1900s.

The Alesbury family
outside Bella Vista house
1904.

Pictured during a Bachelors' Ball in the Town Hall in
the early 1950s are Noel O'Connell, Liam Moran, Seán
O'Connell, Stan Walker, Kitty Moran, and Ann Plunkett.

Barney Byrne, Mr Hope, Ned O'Neill and
Paddy Fitzgerald pictured outside the post
office.

A baby show in the Town Hall in 1954. Among those pictured are Nellie Usher, Cora Usher, Joan Usher, Marie Mangan, Patsy Usher, Lizzie Brereton, Mrs Traynor, Dolores Traynor, Mrs Cleary and Kathleen Cleary.

A section of the crowd at the Bachelors' Dance in the Town Hall, 1956.

Fr Ben Nolan and his sister May, who later became a nun, spent their lives in ministry to God. Edenderry has had many people who joined the priesthood and religious orders.

Bob and Lil Alesbury.

The last group of fourth-class boys who attended the Old Boys' School, or St Joseph's Hall, which was built in 1835 by Revd James Colgan.

Brick Webb, Marcus Loughlin and Dolly Dunne enjoy a drink in O'Donaghue's Pub.

Charles Smith, Bob Goldie and Raymond Tedders, pictured here having a chat in Tedder's Chemist.

Dennis Fay and family, *c.*1895. The Fay family were an integral part of early twentieth-century life at Edenderry.

Dick Mangan of Killane was an influential figure in the formation of the IRA in Edenderry in 1919. Along with others such as Seán O'Ceallaigh and James Colgan, they formed a 'council of elders' to advise young recruits.

Phil Kelly, Frank Caffery, Mary Fanning in the musical *Good Olde Days*, December 1975.

The Dillon Family of Drumcooley pictured in 1935.

Dora Whelan (on the cart) at the tunnel with Ned Shaughnessy, Jack Holt, John Timmons, and Nan, Seán and Eamon O'Neill.

Politics from the pulpit: Fr Kinsella PP of Edenderry (1881–1905) was heavily involved with the Land League, Home Rule and nationalist struggles during his tenure at Edenderry. He ran the wrath of the local Parnellite party in the 1890s because of his opposition to Charles Stewart Parnell. In the early 1900s he asked the Bishop of Kildare and Leighlin to establish a religious order at Edenderry, but opposed the Christian Brothers from being sent to the town.

Frank Burke, Nan Burke and Billy Foran are pictured outisde thier home on Cokery Lane.

Eileen Hickey (*née* Mangan) is pictured here feeding sheep.

Fr John Killian, a popular priest in Edenderry who played an integral role in the development of Edenderry Golf Club.

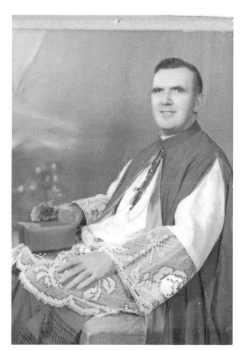

Henry Byrne of Edenderry. Born 18 February 1913, he was ordained a priest in the missionary society of St Columban in 1937. By 1956 he had become Bishop of Iba in the Philippines. He died eight days after resigning as Bishop of Iba on 23 July 1983.

Jeff Kane in Free State Army uniform, early 1920s.

Jimmy Dillon and Mary Logan on their wedding day, 3 February 1914.

Brothers Jimmy and Thomas Kane. During the Irish Civil War, Thomas was shot by Free State troops at Mount Lucas, Daingean. He is buried in Drumcooley cemetery.

Jimmy Rooney, Tom Usher and Jim Usher enjoying a pint and a chat in O'Donaghue's.

John Kelly, Des Farrell, Noel Kelly and Joe Doyle on their way to Mass.

John Greer pictured outside his shop on Fr Kearns Street.

Johnny Timmons of the Tunnel delivers milk into the town. He is pictured here opposite the O'Ceallaigh house on JKL Street.

First Holy Communion Day, 20 May 1961. Front row: Sisters Euphrasia, Remigius, Camillus, Maria Goretti, Ultan, Oliver and Senan. Back row: Sisters Cuthbert, Mother Collette and Bronagh are pictured with Monsignor Martin Brenan and Fr D. O'Sullivan.

Sisters Lorenzo, Calista, Dorothy and Claver.

Another new school year for the staff at Edenderry Girls' National School. Back row: Sisters Euphrasia, Remigius, Alacantra, Maria Goretti, Claver, Ultan, Teresa Joseph, Colmcille, Senan. Front row: Miss Duffy, Sisters Camillus, Oliver, Cuthbert, Colette, Victrine and Miss Moran.

Mother M. de Chantal, Marie Therese and Pauline Jenkins.

Sisters Immaculate, Pauline, [?], and Marie Therese.

James Mangan pictured here with his family at their home on St Francis Street. His bodybuilding and coachworks, which began at the workhouse, prospered in Edenderry for many years.

Maud Augusta Manners was the last of the Manners family to live in Edenderry. Their house was located opposite the Town Hall beside O'Brien's.

Monsignor Martin Brenan on his graduation day in 1923.

Peter and Catherine Ennis pictured in 1885. Originally from Rhode, Ennis was involved in the local Home Rule party in the 1880s, and opposed at elections David Rait Kerr of Rathmoyle.

The Nolan sisters: Clare, Maureen, Monica, Pattie, Kathleen, Joan and Carmel.

A section of the crowd at the Bachelors' Ball in the Town Hall, early 1950s.

Joe Connell, Michael McNally, Henry Hill, Clarence Grey and Guard Brady talking to Tony Malone of Clogherinkoe in Pentony's field in 1957.

Taking a break from delivering the post to the people of Edenderry and the surrounding area are the staff of the Edenderry post office.

Moore's of Edenderry's Meat Van. Their billhead suggested that they served meat to many important people in Ireland, including the Lord Lieutenant, in the early part of the century.

Peter and Mrs O'Neill.

Peter Farrell in action for the Derries Cricket Team.

Peter Farrell and Pearse Usher prior to action with the Derry's Cricket Team.

Liam Moran and Ciaran O'Connell receives a prize in the Edenderry Youth Club Rag Week in 1983 from Majella Cox.

The Reid Family at the grave of Fr Kearns and Col Perry in Monasteroris.

Oliver J. Flanagan, TD for Laois/Offaly, is pictured here at a function to celebrate the restoration of the Town Hall, which had been burned in 1945.

Rosie Tyrell prepares to leave her house at O'Connell Square.

Seán O'Neill, Pat Behan, Nan Tyrell, Fr McWey and Mrs Tyrell.

The Denihan family at their shop on Fr Paul Murphy Street.

The O'Toole family of Kishawanna were wheelwrights for many generations and made many the trap for the people of Edenderry.

Pictured outside the Town Hall are the Edenderry LDF during the Second World War. Fourth row: T. Gowran, P. Connell, F. Foley, S. Nolan, S. Kelly, J. Maguire. Third row: P. Cullen, P. Dempsey, P. Mooney, K. Nolan, T. Davy, T. Grehan, V. Flood, J. Murrin. Second row: E. Moran, P. Connor, H. Butler, P. Slevin, J. Bergin. Front row: B. Byrne, G. Connell, J. Farrelly, P. Forde, T. O'Kennedy, J. Connell, G. Gowran and J. Mullin.

Tom Hussey was a native of Clonard, Co. Meath. He fought in the First World War and lived on Cokery Lane for the remainder of his life.

Charles Manners Jnr and Mary Donegan, accompanied by two others, on a picnic.

Thomas Farrelly at work in his shop on JKL Street.

Hugh Farrell was an important figure in Edenderry in the second half of the nineteenth century. Master of the workhouse, a position he retired from in 1893, he was also an ardent nationalist and wrote a book of poems entitled *Irish National Poems*.

Patrick O'Connor, Maura O'Connell, Eddie Moran and John Keane get ready for a new school year in the Edenderry Boys' National School.

Vin Kelly tells a yarn at the Oakwood Inn.

Joe Mangan and Tom Lawton of 'Midnight Blue' entertain the crowd at the Oakwood Inn.

Ollie Dempsey cleaning windows, a familiar sight throughout Edenderry.

Above: A native of Trim, James Farrelly was an influential figure in Edenderry and throughout the country during the War of Independence, organising local battalions of the IRA.

Right: Joe O'Reilly wrote several books about Edenderry with the help of the children he taught in St Mary's GNS. His work helped preserve the rich folklore that existed in the locality.

Michael McInerney takes a well-earned break to enjoy a cup of tea. For years Michael, originally from Co. Clare, could be seen driving cattle through the main street for Francie Dunne; a sight which like many other things has been lost to progress and a new Ireland.

Thomas and Des Farrell are pictured outside their premises in the square. Farrell's Barber Shop has been in Edenderry for over eighty years.

Left: A young May Patterson. May was one of the founding members of the Edenderry Historical Society.

Right: Thomas Phelan (Rhode) is pictured here in front of Tedder's Chemist in the 1950s.

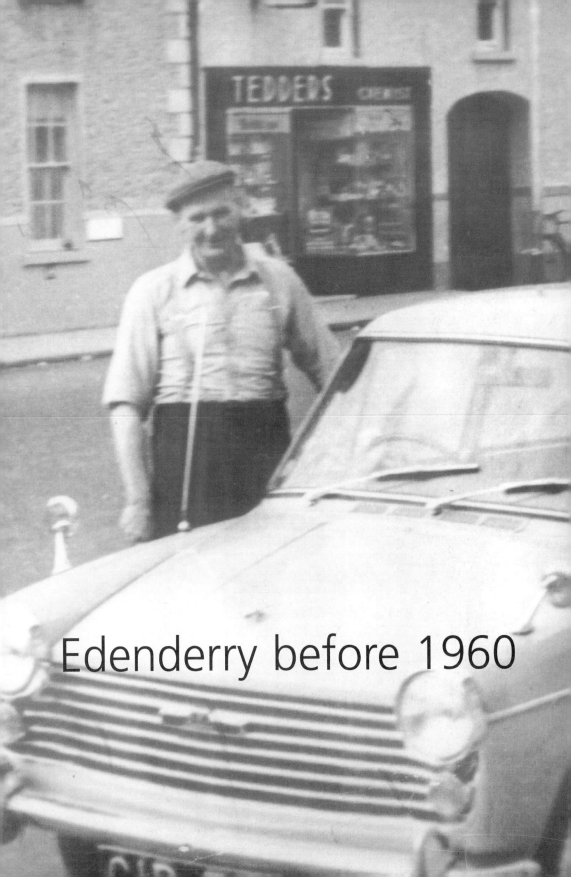

Edenderry before 1960

A panoramic vew of St Mary's church and Edenderry workhouse.

All's quiet along JKL Street in the early 1950s.

Aerial photograph of Edenderry in 1953.

The Central Hotel (where Dermot Hall Menswear is now located in the Square).

Kavanagh's public house, *c.*1940 (now The Corner House – Earl's Bar).

A train arrives in Edenderry on a wet evening in July 1959.

Steve Norman observes the scene on JKL Street.

The interior of St Mary's Roman Catholic church in the late 1950s.

Cattle are driven past Blundell House towards the end of the War of Independence. Blundell House was occupied by the Black and Tans at this time.

The bus arrives in Edenderry, 1933.

Traffic Jam in Edenderry, 1933.

The Harbour on an idle day in 1949.

Looking towards the town pound opposite Edenderry Shoe Factory, 1950s.

O'Shea's Public House (now Finbarr Cullen's) at the turn of the twentieth century.

Laying surface on the road opposite Tedder's in 1943.

A view along Edenderry's main street in 1910.

Looking down St Francis Street, *c.*1900.

Turf Camp at Derries, Edenderry.

The UPS before the fire in 1955.

Flags and bunting adorn the UPS for the procession in 1952.

Rahan House, outside Edenderry, the residence of the Colley Palmer's. It was demolished in 1935.

Nuns outside the Workhouse.

Steam roller gang in the 1940s, laying the road along JKL Street. Includes: Tom Collins, Joe Doyle, Gerry Gorman, Peter Usher, Paddy Dempsey and Jimmy Kane.

People wait outside T. Sheil's Commercial Hotel (now Foy's), early 1900s.

Heading towards Edenderry on the railway line.

Medal given to William Davey for second place in the Handmade Boots category at the Edenderry Industrial Exhibition. 1906. These exhibitions ran from 1905 to 1912.

Workers at Edenderry
Railway Station.

M.P. O'Brien's gasworks at the
Fairgreen established in 1904.

View along JKL Street
from Gibson's shop.

Opposite: Thomas O'Donohoe's was a favourite port of call for all things DIY.

Edenderry towards the present day

Brendan Bergin's butchers and 'Eldorado'.

Brady's supermarket on JKL Street.

Bridge Flanagan's shop beside the Church Walk.

The Oakwood Inn (Byrne's).

The Ulster Bank, flanked by the Man's Shop and Curry Holt's.

Eugene Byrne & Sons Auctioneers.

An aerial view of St Mary's Roman Catholic church built between 1914 and 1918 by Fr Paul Murphy.

Enda Doyle's flower shop.

The Tudor Tavern and Tap Bar.

Attracta Bergin's boutique and the Four County Tavern.

Formerly Moore's house, opposite the Town Hall, now Galileo's Italian Restaurant.

All's quiet on Fr Paul Murphy Street.

Looking down Fr Kearns Street past the Quaker Meeting House.

Looking towards New Row Corner from the Old Boys' School.

One of the oldest houses in the town at New Row Corner, part of what was once the village of Glann.

Golden Fries Italian Restaurant.

Groome's dentist and Kennedy's house.

Holt's Hardware shop, fully equipped in the early 1980s.

Seán T. Farrell's Life and Pensions.

Mangan's Bodybuilding shop supplied vans all across Ireland and beyond.

Along JKL Street in March 1984.

John Reid & Sons. Reid was a renowned photographer, capturing many of the important moments of the twentieth century.

Joyce Farrelly's
knitwear shop at
New Row Corner.

J.P. O'Donnell's shop in O'Connell Square.

Along Col Perry Street
before the 'Celtic Tiger'
claws gave it a facelift.

Kearney's Fabrication when it was located in JKL Street at the family home.

Liam Moran's bicycle shop, an institution in Edenderry for many years.

Tommy Lowry's shop on JKL Street, famed for its fruit and vegetables.

Getting the turf home
for the winter. A tractor
passes through a quiet
Edenderry in 1984.

Houses along JKL
Street opposite
Brady's supermarket,
which have now
been demolished and
rebuilt.

Matsy Mangan's Paper Shop,
where you could rely on a
friendly and efficient service.

Joan Burke walks past McGreal's in March 1984.

The Medical Hall, formerly Kinsella's and now owned by Martin Murphy.

Monica Phelan's front window on JKL Street.

O'Connor's house on JKL Street, beside Eden Bakery.

Damien O'Donaghue's pub on the corner of Fr Kearns Street and Fr P. Murphy Street.

O'Kelly's newsagents located beside the family's home place on JKL Street.

Seán Norman's house, formerly part of the Edenderry Railway Station.

Michael O'Regan's Garage.

Former Offaly footballer Paddy McCormack, 'The Iron man from Rhode', had a public house in the town opposite the Town Hall.

Patrick Larkin's pub on JKL Street. The Larkin's have been publicans and undertakers in Edenderry since 1928.

Pat Reynold's Motor Factors.

Peadar Farrell's Tyre Centre.

Ronan's shop and the ESB office, located close to the harbour.

Ryan's pharmacy, formerly owned by Liam Burke, pictured before the cut was made for Fr McWey Street, part of the most recent development in the town.

Snow falls in Edenderry close to the end of the millennium, in December 1999.

Edenderry in the Twentieth Century

Many events have defined and shaped the history of Edenderry in the twentieth century. The fires at Alesbury's timber factory, the Town Hall, and the Universal Providing Stores were landmark events, as were: the breaches on the canal in 1916 and 1989; the closure of the shoe factory in 1991; the North Strand bombings of 1941, which claimed the lives of the Browne family; the Presidential visits of Seán T. O'Kelly (1950) and Mary Robinson (1994), and the hosting of the National Ploughing championships (1982), amongst other occasions. Despite these trials and tribulations the people and town of Edenderry continued to face adversity on every occasion and to bounce back when the odds were stacked against them. Any history is but a sprinkling of collections of times past, and sadly some people or events may have gone unrecorded. To the men and women of Edenderry and those who came to call Edenderry their new home in the twentieth century, we owe a great debt. As twenty-first-century Edenderry takes a new shape and look, we remember the past and those who contributed to the development of our town.

Politically Edenderry has been under-represented since Ireland gained its independence in 1922. Those who went to the poll from Edenderry for a Dáil seat include Andrew Byrne and Seán O'Ceallaigh (1923), Andrew Fay (1927), George Connell (1943), Frank Byrne (1957), Ger Killaly (1997 and 2002) and John Foley (2007). Only one candidate was elected – Eugene P. O'Brien in February 1932 representing the Cumman Na Gaedhael party and receiving 3,713 votes. O'Brien, however only served ten months in the Dáil, during which time he spoke on six occasions in the house, never on issues related to Edenderry.

Three fires had a profound effect on the history of Edenderry in the twentieth century. These were: the blaze at Alesbury's timber factory in June 1904 causing £30,000 worth of damage and putting 150 men out of work; the Town Hall fire in January 1945 which, only for the valiant efforts of 'Smokey' the dog, may have had tragic consequences (he awoke the O'Connell family who were living in the building), and the burning of the Universal Providing Stores, O'Brien's in August 1955, of which this collection contains a number of images.

The 1960s saw the end of the canal and railway at Edenderry being used for commercial and passenger traffic to Dublin. The railway had been a vital communication network with Dublin since it opened in 1877 under the patronage of Miss Downing Nesbitt of Tubberdaly House, Rhode. Special trains were organised in the early 1960s for GAA matches such as the Leinster and All-Ireland finals involving the Offaly GAA teams. Sadly, transport on the Grand

Canal ceased operations around the same time; the last barge left in 1960. Today barges still visit the town and create a wonderful amenity and pastime for both tourist and local alike. Many people in Edenderry will remember the canal breach of January 1989 and the destruction and inundation that it caused on the land surrounding it. Major breaches on the Grand Canal have occurred at Edenderry on three occasions in the nineteenth century, and also in 1916 and in 1989. The repair work on the canal in 1916 was disrupted by snow drifts which delayed the work for almost a fortnight. On this occasion an English scientist visited Edenderry and claimed that earthquake tremors measured off the coast of England may have been the cause of this breach. Throughout the 1990s the OPW have worked to repair the bank wall of the canal at the harbour which flows into Edenderry. The closure of Alesbury timber factory in September 1931 had a profound effect on the locality. Indeed the issue was disputed for many months, during which time the town witnessed many strikes and angry scenes between workers and management. The issue was even raised in the Dáil and angry exchanges ensued between TDs Seán Lemass and Patrick McGilligan. The newspapers of the day reported that the situation had become so volatile that when the last orders were being made in the factory, police protection was needed as angry locals threatened to destroy the goods.

Following the industrial unrest of the early 1930s, Seán Lemass, Minister for Industry and Commerce, secured for Edenderry in 1935 the opening of the Irish Shoe Company under the direction of Norman Wachman. The shoe company employed as many as 500 at its peak and was a severe blow to the locality when it closed in 1991. Some of the images of the town of Edenderry contained in this volume were taken on a day in March 1984 when the signage on O'Brien's was taken down, ending nearly 150 years of the family's association with Edenderry. It signalled an end of an era for the people of the town and the surrounding areas who had come to see O'Brien's as a way of life, where personal service and expertise were offered when they did their shopping in the store. The O'Brien empire, which included shops in Allenwood, Kilmeague, Maynooth and Tullow, traded on the slogan that they stocked 'everything from an anchor to a needle'. Quinnsworth replaced O'Brien's in Edenderry and with it a new era in shopping began.

'If you seek a monument, look around', reads the inscription on the grave of Fr Paul Murphy, the most popular priest if not individual during the twentieth century at Edenderry. Fr Murphy had come to Edenderry in 1910 when he quickly realised the dilapidated state of the parish church at Killane. So he commenced building a new church. The church was built between 1914 and 18, during the Great War, the stone brought from Tullamore by the O'Neill brothers amongst others. Money was gathered by any means possible and when this church was finally consecrated by the Bishop of Kildare and Leighlin in 1932 it had been completely paid for. Fr Murphy incurred the wrath of the local R.I.C. during the War of Independence when he was suspected of being in sympathy with the Republican cause and with the locals during the Treaty debates, when he openly spoke out from the altar against the Anglo-Irish agreement signed by Michael Collins and the Irish delegation.

Other priests in the area that influenced life at Edenderry in the twentieth century included Fr John Killian and Monsignor Martin Brenan. The Golf Club and its growth owe much to the service of Fr Killian, noted for travelling on horseback. Monsignor Martin Brenan was a native of Castlecomer, Co. Kilkenny and was ordained a priest in Maynooth in 1926. He became a professor of Education and Catechetics in 1931 and became President of Carlow

College in 1949. He died on 4 March 1982 having been parish priest of Edenderry. His many published works include *The Schools of Kildare and Leighlin* (1935). However, pride of place in the hearts of many people in Edenderry must surely go to Fr John McWey, parish priest from 1951 to 1976. Renowned for his kindness and faith, Fr McWey immersed himself in every part of life in Edenderry, from the GAA to Muintir na Tíre. His grave in the grounds of Kilcock church, where he spent the last years of his life, is still a place of pilgrimage for many from Edenderry who believe in the healing ways of the Laois-born priest. The history of Edenderry and in particular Castro Petre church was well preserved by Archdeacon Charles Finney, who published a book in 1978 while ministering in the area.

The twentieth century at Edenderry has seen success in every sport. The great Edenderry 'Reds' of the 1950s and late 1990s brought success on the football fields, while All-Ireland hurling medals were won by Finbarr Cullen (minor 1989), Seán Og Farrell (senior 1994) and Cillian Farrell (senior 1998). All-Ireland football medals were brought to the parish in 1971/72 by Seán Evans and in 1982 by Gerry Carroll. Edenderry Rugby Club has also enjoyed the success of Provincial Towns Cup triumphs in 1967 and 1983, while similarly Edenderry Town Soccer Club has gone from strength to strength over the years, and owes much to the tireless efforts of men such as Paddy Maloney. Boxing has also been a popular sport in Edenderry, even before independence in 1922. The highlights for the club over the years must surely include the visit of Muhammed Ali to Croke Park in 1972 in which Seán Brereton was responsible for erecting the ring. That event was eclipsed some eight years later, however, when in 1980 Seán's son Martin competed in the Olympic Games in Moscow where he fought against Jose Aguilar of Cuba. Many of the images in this collection recall sporting triumphs and loss on the cricket fields, a sport which proved very popular in Edenderry up until the 1960s. The members of Edenderry Golf Club have enjoyed considerable success over the years and continue to improve their facilities. Since 1992, Highfield Golf Club has also provided excellent facilities for golfers. Other clubs and societies such as the Canoe Club, the Youth Club, the Boy Scouts and Cubs are no longer in existence but did provide an excellent outlet for the youth of Edenderry over the years.

Michael Murphy's excellent history of the Edenderry Towns Commissioners, *Edenderry: A Leinster town*, offers an insight into the people who have administered the town's commission since it began in 1908. In the early years, figures like M.P. O'Brien, Andrew Byrne and Seán O' Ceallaigh dominated the proceedings. Much of the business of the twentieth century revolved around Jim Flanagan, the longest-serving town commissioner in Ireland, Molly Earley the town clerk and Eileen O'Connor. The commissioners have worked tirelessly for the town of Edenderry which sadly has been misrepresented at county and national level. As many people realise, with limited resources and limited power, the Edenderry Towns Commissioners have achieved much in their one-hundred-year existence.

The town of Edenderry has been privileged to have the President of Ireland visit the town on two occasions in the twentieth century. In 1950, the visit of Seán T. O'Kelly coincided with the second visit of Cardinal Gilroy to Edenderry. On this occasion Seán T. O'Kelly invoked the spirit of 1798 when he spoke to the crowd, reminding them that the people of Edenderry were always ready to do their part for the cause of old Ireland. In June 1994 the first female President of Ireland, Mary Robinson addressed the people of Edenderry and unveiled plaques at historic locations in the town commissioned by the historical society. On various occasions the town has witnessed visits from other major national figures, such as the 1934 visit of the leader of the

Blueshirts, Eoin O'Duffy who spoke at a gymkhana organised by the local branch of the Fine Gael party. The visits of Cardinal Gilroy, the Bishop of Adelaide, were the highlights in the late 1940s for the people of Edenderry in what was a time of economic crisis and depression. The houses built in Gilroy Avenue were named in his honour, and retain a link to the past. Other important events staged at Edenderry included the National Ploughing Championships, which were held in October 1982 on the land of Alec Tong, at a time when the town and county were still celebrating Seamus Darby's goal that ended Kerry's 'five in a row' hopes in the All-Ireland Football final.

In 1929, Mass was celebrated at Monasteroris for the first time in over 300 years. It had been organised by Fr Paul Murphy and the Franciscan Order of Friars. The Mass was held to celebrate the centenary of Catholic Emancipation brought about in 1829 by the 'Great Liberator', Daniel O'Connell. In 1927/28 the hinterlands of the town of Edenderry saw new owners of the soil, on estates which had been broken up by the Irish Land Commission. These 'Kerry migrants' as the newspapers of the time called them, had come from impoverished lands in the 'Kingdom', from the Dingle peninsula and Castleisland. Families such as the Fitzgeralds, the O'Connor's and the Evans settled into life at Edenderry and have been integral members of the community ever since. The development of the bogs around Edenderry, the hinterland of the great bog of Allen, by Bord Na Mona since the mid-1940s was the single most important factor in the development of Edenderry over the last hundred years. The bogs provided employment for the local people and attracted people from all across the country, many of whom settled and made Edenderry their new home. The dances and balls which were organised for workers in the turf camps were for many the social highlight of the year and are fondly remembered by those who attended them.

With the outbreak of the Second World War, Ireland remained neutral but the threat posed by both belligerents, the United Kingdom and Germany meant that local defence forces known as the LDF were formed. Edenderry proudly played its part in this. During the war years, which were times of economic hardship for the country, the drilling, marching and parades were a source of entertainment for the locals and pride for those who took part in them. The LDF in Edenderry drilled and paraded regularly and carried out reconnaissance missions, exchanging information weekly at Ballymacwilliam with the LDF unit from Rhode. But the Second World War was a time of sadness for the people of Edenderry after the bombing of Dublin's North Strand on 31 May 1941, which claimed the lives of the Browne family, formerly of Edenderry. On 4 June 1941 the bodies of Harry Browne, his wife Molly, his mother Mary and their four children, Maureen, Ann, Edward and Angela were brought to Edenderry on the back of an O'Brien's lorry and buried in Drumcooley Cemetery. In all, thirty-four people were killed in the North Strand bombings.

The images contained in this volume are but a sample of life in Edenderry in the twentieth century. It is hoped that another volume of photographs will follow this, as over 600 were received and scanned by the society over the past year. The foregoing notes will act as a guide to the some of the images featured in the volume. If they provoke conversation, debate and reminiscences then they will surely have achieved their primary function. While it has not been possible to identify every person in every photograph, perhaps readers may fill the missing blanks where necessary. The society welcomes your comments.